Juno Dawson

Published in paperback in Great Britain in 2019 by Wayland

ISBN: 978 1 5263 0001 0
10 9 8 7 6 5 4 3 2 1

Printed in Dubai

Wayland
An imprint of
Hachette Children's Group
Part of Hodder & Stoughton
Carmelite House
50 Victoria Embankment
London EC4Y 0DZ
An Hachette UK Company
www.hachette.co.uk
www.hachettechildrens.co.uk

Editor: Sarah Silver
Designer: Rocket Design (East Anglia) Ltd
Cover design: Oli Frape

Picture acknowledgements: John Arehart/Shutterstock: 41cl. Chubykin Arkady/Shutterstock: 20t. Pasha Barabanov/Shutterstock: 34-35. Beeboys/Shutterstock: 6t. Sam Beeson and Latifu Laye via the contributor Anthony Anaxagorou: 23. BlueRingMedia/Shutterstock: 6c, 6b. L. Bourne via the contributor Holly Bourne: 5cr, 31. Alice Che/Shutterstock: 25t. Creatista/Shutterstock: 14t. CRS Photo/Shutterstock: 35tr. Via the contributor Juno Dawson: 16t, 17. Via the contributor Laura Dockrill: 22. Scott Dudelson/Getty Images: 15b. Everett Art/Shutterstock: 18. Everett Historical/Shutterstock: 28. Lee Faircloth via the contributer Matt Lister: 38, 39. Featureflash Photo Agency/Shutterstock: 13, 15t. Kay Fiáin via the contributor Krishna Istha: 5cl, 42. Franck Fife/Getty Images: 9b. Jonathan Hordle/REX/Shutterstock: 41r. Ovidiu Hrubaru/Shutterstock: 9t, 30. Kathy Hutchins/Shutterstock: 24, 36b, 45. Jaguar PS/Shutterstock: 29b, 40. Kansas City Star/Getty Images: 25b. Sharon Kilgannon via the contributor Fox Fisher: 5bl. 26, 27. Paul Kingsley/Alamy: 35b. Kateryna Kon/Shutterstock: 7b. kryzhov/Shutterstock: 7c. Alexey Kuznetsov/Shutterstock: 14b. Mark Miller/Wikimedia Commons: 34b. Brian Minkoff /Shutterstock: 33b. PictureGroup/REX/Shutterstock: 33t. Stas Ponomarencko/Shutterstock: 21b. project 1 photography/Shutterstock: 19tl. Rawpixel.com/Shutterstock: 36c. Gent Shkullaku/Getty Images: 35tl. Urszula Soltys via the contributor Andrew McMillan: 5br, 43. J Stone/Shutterstock: 19r, 21t, 32. Tinseltown/Shutterstock: 29t. vector brothers/Shutterstock: 37b. Fam Veld/Shutterstock: 11, 20b. Donna Ward/Getty Images: 5t. Emily Marie Wilson/Shutterstock: 15c. Debby Wong/Shutterstock: 41t.

Every attempt has been made to clear copyright. Should there be any inadvertent omission, please apply to the publisher for rectification.

The website addresses (URLs) included in this book were valid at the time of going to press. However, it is possible that contents or addresses may have changed since the publication of this book. No responsibility for any such changes can be accepted by either the author or the Publisher.

Contents

Introducing gender

When couples are expecting a baby, the first question people often ask them is 'are you having a boy or a girl?' Easy enough to answer, right? After all, the world is divided into two types of human: males and females. It is thought that 49.6% of the world's population is female and 50.4% is male. So far, so good. But what if it isn't quite that straightforward? A person's sex and their gender are very different things, and that's where this identity business can get complicated.

Why do we need this book?

You've probably heard words like 'gender', 'sex', 'man', 'woman', 'boy', 'girl', 'lady' or 'gentleman' and not really thought too much about what they mean. But they *are* important. This is because both your sex and your gender are having an impact on your life *and* your future, even if you aren't particularly aware of it.

Gender is how you feel, and this feeling may not necessarily be the same as your sex. Your gender will influence how other people see you. People might make entirely false assumptions about you based on nothing more than whether you're a boy or a girl. For some people,

being the gender they are given at birth makes them happy, for others it makes them quite sad.

In society, depending on where you are in the world, your gender might mean you have very different options, choices and prospects. It is important we discuss something that affects people's lives as much as gender does.

THINK ABOUT

Why does it matter whether you're a boy or a girl?

> " The problem with gender is that it prescribes how we should be rather than recognising how we are. Now imagine how much happier we would be, how much freer, to be our true individual selves if we didn't have the weight of gender expectations. "

CHIMAMANDA NGOZI ADICHIE, AUTHOR

How this book works

By the end of this book, you'll have learned several things:

- The *difference between sex and gender*
- *What it means to be transgender*
- The *difference between sex and sexuality*
- *What the term 'genderfluid' means*
- *What are sexism and feminism*
- *Why we need better equality.*

If you can tick off everything on that list, I've done my job!

You'll also hear from super-cool, clever people (like the ones pictured here, and more!) who all have something to say about their personal gender philosophies.

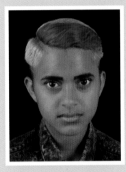

Krishna Istha explains what it means to be multi-gendered.

Find out what **Holly Bourne** thinks about feminism.

Fox Fisher tells their experience of being transgender.

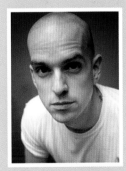

Read a poem by **Andrew McMillan** about gender identity.

What is sex?

When you were born, it's highly likely a doctor or a midwife proudly announced 'congratulations! You have a bouncing baby _____!'

This proclamation was almost certainly based on what they observed between your legs. This is your sex and not necessarily your gender – more on that later.

Sex

Sex is based on five key features of your biology:

1. External genitals – This is the bit the doctor or midwife could see. Females have a clitoris, vulva and labia, while males have a penis and scrotum.

2. Internal genitals – In order to reproduce (make babies), males and females have different anatomy inside their abdomen. Females have a vagina, uterus and fallopian tubes while males have a prostate and tubes for the sperm to travel through.

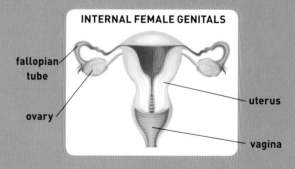

INTERNAL FEMALE GENITALS

fallopian tube

ovary

uterus

vagina

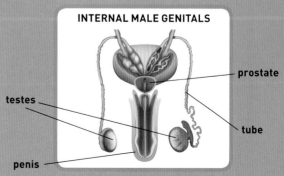

INTERNAL MALE GENITALS

prostate

testes

tube

penis

3. Sex organs – Females have ovaries, which release an egg once a month if she is of reproductive age (roughly from age 12 to 49). Testes, the male sex organs, produce sperm. Sex organs are also called 'gonads'.

4. Hormones – Hormones are chemical messengers that tell our body to do all sorts of things like 'be hungry' or 'be tired'. Our bodies are all full of the same hormones, but levels will vary between males and females. Females produce more of the hormone oestrogen and progesterone, while males tend to have more of the hormone testosterone.

5. Chromosomes – sex chromosomes (in your genes) are clever little things which tell the rest of your body to develop typically male or typically female characteristics. Female mammals have two X chromosomes, males have one X and one Y. Of course, a doctor can't see that unless he or she is looking under a powerful microscope.

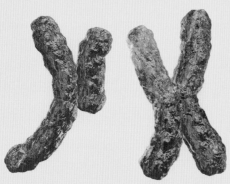

HIGHLY MAGNIFIED X AND Y CHROMOSOMES

Why is sex important?

Sex is important for one BIG reason: reproduction. Humans create babies through a process called sexual reproduction. In humans, a male provides a seed to fertilise a female egg that then develops in a female uterus for nine months.

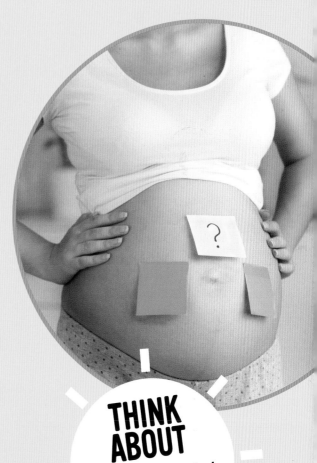

THINK ABOUT

Do you know what someone's sex is just by looking at them?

What is intersex?

A person is said to be intersex if they are born with characteristics of both sexes or are sexually ambiguous somehow (that means the doctor or midwife can't immediately tell by looking between a baby's legs). Does this make the baby a boy or a girl? It can be a difficult issue.

Defining intersex

Because there are so many different ways for a baby to be classed as intersex, it's very hard to say for certain how many intersex people there are in the world, but it's *probably* somewhere around 1% of all births. That's as many people as have red hair!

Sometimes, if a baby is born with elements of both male and female genitals, parents choose to have surgery to fix the 'problem'. This is very controversial, however, as a baby has no say in whether they *feel* more like a girl or a boy.

When they are old enough, many intersex people choose whether they most identify as a man, woman, or describe themselves as transgender or intersex.

THINK ABOUT

Who do you think should decide about intersex surgery? Individuals, doctors, parents, judges or someone else?

Hanne Gaby Odiele

Hanne is a Dutch supermodel who was born intersex. Her parents decided to allow doctors to operate on her as a baby, a decision that Hanne disagrees with. 'I have reached a point in my life where I feel ready to share this important part of who I am,' she said when she 'came out' as intersex. 'It is time for intersex people to come out of the shadows, claim our status, let go of shame, and speak out against the unnecessary and harmful surgeries many of us were subjected to as children. Intersex children born today are still at risk for these human rights violations. I will use my voice and platform to help end such abuses.'

Caster Semenya

Caster is a super-talented South African Olympic medallist. Her case highlights how cruel some people can be about gender. After winning the 800 m competition at the 2009 World Championships in Athletics, speculation started about her gender – with some people in the media and athletics suggesting she had been 'born male' or was intersex, and that her victory wasn't fair. In the end, Caster was allowed to keep her medals and she was allowed a right to privacy about her sex.

THINK ABOUT

Why is privacy a human right?

What is gender?

If sex is biological, then gender is anything but. Biologically we have — if we're being very simplistic — two sexes: male and female. Well, male, female and intersex, as we've already seen. Gender is different. Gender is about your identity.

THE OFFICIAL DEFINITION

'Gender refers to the socially constructed characteristics of women and men – such as norms, roles and relationships of and between groups of women and men. It varies from society to society and can be changed.'

The World Health Organisation (WHO)

Gosh! There's a lot to break down there, isn't there? What does that actually mean?

Socially constructed – That means gender is characteristics we have made up. They are 'rules' that we have chosen, not really based on any facts. They may be linked to biology or science, but there's a lot more to it than that.

Norms, roles and relationships – This means what's considered 'normal' things or behaviours for men and women or boys and girls to do.

It varies from society to society – Something that we think is 'normal' for men or women in the UK, might seem very strange in another part of the world.

It can be changed – This means gender is a flexible, or changeable characteristic. An individual isn't necessarily 'stuck' with the gender they've been given at birth and gender norms can change over time. For example, even fifty years ago it would have been rare for a girl to go to university or for a boy to become a nurse but now it's no big deal.

> **" Gender is between your ears, not between your legs. "**
>
> **CHAZ BONO, ACTOR**

THINK ABOUT

How would you explain 'gender' to your friends?

Sugar and spice and all things nice,
that's what little girls are made of.
Slime and snails and puppy dogs' tails,
that's what little boys are made of.

TRADITIONAL NURSERY RHYME

What are 'gender norms'?

If sex is to do with bits of your body, gender is everything else. When we think of 'gender norms' we are talking about the following things:

- *Your name – some names are usually given to boys (David, Muhammad), some are usually given to girls (Sarah, Eve) and some are quite gender neutral (Sam, Alex)*

- *Your pronouns ('he', 'his', 'she', 'her', 'their')*

- *The clothes you wear*

- *Your hair*

- *Make-up*

- *The toys you have*

- *Your school uniform*

- *The box you tick on a form*

- *The sports you do in PE*

- *Hobbies*

- *Colours (pink and blue are the most obvious examples).*

What are gender stereotypes?

You tell me! On a piece of paper, see if you can list twenty stereotypes about boys and twenty about girls.

A STEREOTYPE is another word for characteristics or assumptions about a group of people. These ideas about people can come from our own experiences, from our family and friends and from books, films and other media. Stereotypes are different all around the world and they can change over time.

THINK ABOUT

Look at your list. Why do you think these stereotypes might be unfair?

Expectations in gender

Gender is so tricky because it's all very much a matter of opinion. Like, why is long hair for girls? Why is blue for boys? People might *expect* boys to behave in a certain way and girls to behave in a different way, but that's not really very fair.

The stereotypes of boys being rough, tough and masculine and girls being pretty, delicate and feeble are certainly not always true, and they can restrict us from doing things we really want to.

Be who you want to be

Some girls will be very 'girly' and that's fine. Some boys are very 'masculine' and that's fine too. The problem is when boys and girls feel like they *don't* live up to expectations set out by gender stereotypes. It can make you feel like you're 'getting it wrong'.

Girls might feel like they have to look a certain way or be nice, polite and agreeable. Boys might feel that they can't show emotion or cry when they're upset. Gender stereotypes are damaging for both boys and girls.

However, there is no 'right way' to be a boy or a girl.

You really can't go wrong. It doesn't matter what you wear; the toys you play with; how you speak or how you behave. As long you aren't hurting anyone else in the process, the most important thing is to be who you are. You are also free to be friends with boys *and* girls. It is fine if you are a girl who likes hanging out with boys and vice versa.

" *Only the individual person is important. Everybody should be free to live life as he or she sees fit, as long as nobody gets harmed.* "

CONCHITA WURST / TOM NEUWIRTH, SINGER

THINK ABOUT

Where do you think gender stereotypes come from?

Mums and dads

Traditional ideas about what mothers and fathers should do are also very stereotypical. As recently as fifty or sixty years ago, and especially before the Second World War, it was true that most mothers stayed at home to cook, clean and look after the children while fathers went out to work. But, as we already know, gender norms change over time and these traditional ideas are not always true any longer.

Today many women go back to work after they've had children. Some fathers now stay at home to cook, clean and look after the children. However, studies show that women still tend to do more household chores than men.

It's also now very common for a child to have two mothers or two fathers. These can either be step-parents or same-sex couples. Families come in all different shapes and sizes.

THINK ABOUT

Is it fair that women do more housework than men? Who does most of the housework in your home?

> **"** I love a challenge. And I love defying limitation, gender stereotypes, and people's expectations of me ... **"**

GWENDOLINE CHRISTIE, ACTOR

Do what you want to do

Firefighter, ballet dancer, builder, nurse. What gender comes to mind when you read each of these jobs? Traditionally in society, people have thought there are jobs that are better for men to do, and jobs that are better for women to do. But your gender doesn't determine how good you are at something and the skills you can learn. There are many very successful female firefighters, and male nurses. So don't let your gender get in the way of your dreams!

YOUR GENDER DOESN'T DEFINE WHAT YOU CAN AND CAN'T DO.

THINK ABOUT

How can we change gender stereotypes?

> **"** I always say I never felt 'latched' to a gender. I just kind of always felt like myself, and I never felt like I had to do certain things or be a certain way to fit into a certain mould. **"**

SHAMIR, SINGER-SONGWRITER

My gender:

Juno Dawson

So who am I and why am I so interested in gender? When I was very little — like three or four years old — I was pretty much certain that I was a little girl. It's my earliest memory. But there was one problem: when I was born my parents were told I was a boy.

Growing up

My parents called me James and treated me like I was a boy. This meant I had gender very much thrust on me. Lots of times I got told off for not behaving the way a little boy 'should'. I wasn't allowed to play with the toys I wanted to play with or wear the clothes I wanted to wear.

❝ It was super frustrating and, every night before I went to sleep, I used to pray that I'd be a girl when I woke up in the morning. It didn't work out like that. ❞

Finding out

A long, long time later, when I was a grown up, I learned that a lot of people change their gender and elements of their sex too. These people are called transgender, or sometimes transsexuals. I spoke to lots of transgender people, my family, a therapist and a doctor and realised that I was transgender too.

Transitioning

I started my gender transition from James to Juno in my early thirties. At first, you change your outward appearance: I changed my hair, my clothes, my name, my passport and everyone started to call me 'she' and 'her'. Later, I started to take hormones that will also eventually change my body. In the future I might also have various operations to make my face and body more female-looking too. My mum, dad and sister have been very supportive and helped me as I've made changes in my life.

Being myself

I feel a lot more like 'myself' since starting my transition. It has made me happier, although transitioning can be very hard work. Sometimes people on the street or on trains laugh at me or say unkind things and that is very hurtful. Still, I think that sort of mean behaviour says more about them than it does about me, don't you? I think I should have always been a woman, and now I'm doing something about it.

Why do boys and girls look different?

Once boys and girls go through puberty into adulthood, their bodies will look increasingly different.

Comparing gender

Men tend to be taller, heavier, have greater lung capacity, and broader shoulders than women. Men can usually grow facial hair and body hair. Women tend to have wider hips and have breasts. To get technical, we call these 'secondary sexual characteristics'.

But it's impossible to say 'this is what men look like' or 'this is what women look like'. Some women are very tall, some men aren't. Some women don't have large breasts and some men don't have broad shoulders. In films or in magazines, we tend to see the same sort of stereotypical, tanned, slender bodies, but that doesn't mean there's only one way to 'look like' a man or woman.

Are there gender rules?

In terms of hair, clothes and make-up – these things are purely gender. Some people say that certain items like skirts or make-up are just for women, but different cultures have different 'norms' about how men and women should look.

IN THE EIGHTEENTH CENTURY, IT WAS VERY TRENDY FOR MEN TO WEAR FLOWING, POWDERED WIGS.

Up until the early nineteenth century, pink clothes were worn equally often by men and women. In fact, pink was MORE popular for boys because soldiers often wore red and pink! In ancient Rome, Greece and Egypt it was the norm for men to wear skirts. Scottish men wear skirts, known as kilts, on special occasions.

SARONGS, VESHTIS AND MUNDUS ARE ALSO WORN BY MEN THROUGHOUT ASIA.

Men have worn make-up since ancient times to represent status. Ancient Romans wore face paint to cover bald spots.

So you see, the 'rules' about how boys and girls are 'meant' to look are really a load of made-up nonsense! No one can say what we'll all be wearing in ten, twenty or thirty years' time because society, culture and fashion are constantly evolving.

There are so many conflicting ideas about what you should and shouldn't wear, the only sensible thing to do is dress precisely how you want to dress and ignore 'the rules'!

" In this society, if a man is called a woman, that's the biggest insult he could get. Is that because women are considered something less? "

ANDREJA PEJIĆ, SUPERMODEL

THINK ABOUT

Other than clothes, make-up and hair, what other things are 'just for boys' or 'just for girls'?

Why can't boys play with dolls?

Well, of course, boys CAN play with dolls, and many of them do. The problem is that some people might make fun of them for doing so.

Child's play

When boys play with traditionally female toys, they get called 'sissies' or other mean names, while girls who play traditionally boys' games get called 'tomboys'. That sort of name-calling is not cool. Often, until children start to tease each other, everyone plays with the dolls in the home area at primary school.

Activity time!

Make a chart with two columns – one of boys' toys and games and one of girls' toys and games. List as many activities as you can think of.

I imagine the boys' column is full of aggressive, noisy, physical activities, such as football and computer games while the girls' side is full of lovely, caring and nurturing games, such as playing with dolls and making crafts. Am I right?

Children should be encouraged to play with all different sorts of toys. We want both boys *and* girls to be creative, physical, competitive, caring and imaginative. Children should be allowed to play with whatever toys they like.

There is a popular campaign called 'Let Toys Be Toys' which aims to stop toy shops from advertising toys as 'boys' toys' or 'girls' toys' and just let children pick the things they want to play with. Some toy shops no longer have different sections for girls and boys.

What we have to do is challenge stereotypes about both boys and girls.

" No-one has ever been able to tell me I couldn't do something because I was a girl. "

ANNE HATHAWAY, ACTOR

THINK ABOUT

Who teaches children which toys are for boys and which are for girls?

My gender:
Laura Dockrill

Laura Dockrill is an acclaimed British poet and author.

Being a kid

I've always been slightly aware that I wasn't a girly girl. Or that I wasn't interested in being one either. I owe lots to my parents, they did a really good job of not objectifying my brother, sister and I for our looks but letting us just be kids. I could be a boy or girl but I could also be a spider or a mermaid or a superhero or a vampire.

Gender in writing

I feel the job of a writer is to feed life and breath into a voice, mostly one from our imaginations. I like to write for boys and girls but also be voices from the past and future. One of the coolest things about my job is asking myself: *I wonder what it would be like to be ...*

Stretching the imagination

I find it really unfair when people challenge writers on their fictional representations of characters. Often there is a lot of 'How would you know how it feels to be ...' But that's our job, to explore and investigate, to give breath and depth and create characters that haven't yet been surfaced. I get more stick for writing from the point of view of a boy than I do a mermaid. And I am pretty sure I can stretch my imagination to conjure up what life is like for a 16-year-old boy much easier than a mutant half monster-fish woman living a life of magic underwater. I love it when I see a well-written male or female and it's written by the other sex. I think that's great.

My gender:

Anthony Anaxagorou

Anthony Anaxagorou is a performance poet who grew up in London, UK.

Feeling pain

I remember playing with my younger brother when I was nine years old. We were trying to climb a tree but my brother slipped and cut open his knee. My dad heard him crying and came running to see what had happened. After a quick inspection he could see it was only a minor cut so he told him firmly to be a man and stop crying. At that point, I remember thinking how the ways I'd responded to pain defined my manliness. I felt almost embarrassed for ever having felt a sense of hurt. Maybe I was a girl? I looked closer at the scratches I'd accumulated climbing trees and fighting with my cousins then instantly felt tougher for not having cried out like my brother.

Being emotional

I had to become more confident within myself before I could dismiss conventional ideas of masculinity and manliness. Allowing myself to be emotional and sensitive was probably the first step despite the men in my family insisting I had to 'man up' or grow a 'thicker skin.' I've learnt how to articulate reasons why boys and men should be encouraged to express their emotions in all the ways they wish. When I speak to young adults they often associate emotion with women and strength with men. We can be both. We are both. The sooner we allow ourselves to be vulnerable and confused and sad, the quicker we will get to becoming secure and happy within ourselves.

What is
transgender?

" There's a gender in your brain and a gender in your body. For 99 per cent of people, those things are in alignment. For transgender people, they're mismatched. **"**

CHAZ BONO, ACTOR

Getting it right

Sometimes, people (like me!) do not agree with the gender they were assigned at birth.

I admit it's a bit of a head scratcher isn't it? How can someone 'feel' they ought to be a boy or a girl? How can any of us know 'what it feels like' to be a girl or a boy? Nonetheless a lot of people – from a very young age – just feel Mother Nature, or God, or biology, or fate GOT IT WRONG. Trans people feel their mind and their body do not 'match'.

There are as many ways to be transgender as there are transgender people:

- SOME trans people will change their name and their pronouns – meaning they might now use 'he' instead of 'she' or vice versa. Some people use 'they' or 'ze' if they don't feel that 'he' or 'she' is appropriate.

- SOME trans people might change the clothes they wear.

- SOME trans people might take hormone medication to change the shape of their body.

- SOME trans people might have operations to change their bodies further.

SHE, HER PLEASE.

HE, HIS PLEASE.

THEY, THEIR PLEASE.

How to be trans

Being transgender is a very personal thing. You really can't 'get it wrong'. Transition can be a slow process that takes many years and a trans person is never 'finished'. For example, many trans people will be taking hormone medication for the rest of their lives.

You've probably seen stories in the news about 'transgender children'. Some young people might decide they want to transition while they are still children (in law, this means under the age of 18).

These young people will be given support, counselling and sometimes medication until they are old enough to make adult decisions about changing their gender on a more permanent basis.

Trans men and trans women are like any other men or women in society. The only significant difference is that trans women cannot get pregnant. They are, of course, able to foster, adopt or use surrogate parents, just like lots of people do.

Avery Jackson

Avery Jackson is a transgender girl who shared her experience of transition on YouTube.

'When I was born, doctors said I was a boy, but I knew in my heart I was a girl. So I may have some boy body parts, but that's not wrong. That is okay. [...] Being transgender is a hard thing but you can be who you want to be.'

My gender:

Fox Fisher

Fox Fisher is an artist, filmmaker and one of the stars of the TV documentary My Transsexual Summer.

A tomboy

I was assigned female at birth, but never really connected to that. There was no awareness of trans people when I was growing up so I never realised it was possible for me to identify as a boy. I was considered a tomboy, because I used to play with the boys, and wear male clothing. I was also considered a 'black sheep' and a rebel in my family because I wouldn't conform and always got upset about being forced into feminine clothing or for being too boisterous.

Time to change

I spent a lot of my childhood depressed and a lot of my early adulthood was spent feeling very lost indeed. Eventually, I realised that the only thing that would change my panic attacks and feelings of deep sadness was a social and medical transition.

Feeling scared

I realised the biggest thing holding me back was myself. I was so scared of telling people how I felt. I didn't think anyone would take me seriously and I wasn't sure if this would even help me to fill the void. I was scared that I could go through the whole process (name change, hormones, surgery) and perhaps it wouldn't ease the deep sense of unhappiness. I felt annoyed that I needed to change my body in order to be happy. Why couldn't I just love my skinny androgynous body and be happy being seen as a girl?

My journey

But I couldn't live any longer being treated as a female. It felt like a lie. At this point I had nothing to lose. So I started my journey, changing my name, my documents, going to the doctor and then starting hormones and having surgery. Luckily, taking hormones and being treated as 'other than female' made me feel so much better and I realised it was worth the risk. I wished I had done it sooner.

Being me

I'm so happy with my life now. I can help others now that I've sorted my own issues and I feel so proud to be part of the trans community. It's such a pleasure to no longer feel constantly distressed and strange in my own skin. I love exploring what it means to be 'me' and helping others to feel better about themselves through the films I create.

Gender
and feminism

Earlier on, I said that your gender will have an impact on your life. This is especially true for women. As crazy as it seems, for a very, very long time women didn't have as many rights in society as men. That means they weren't allowed to vote in elections; earn equal pay; go out to work; make decisions about who they marry or whether or not they wanted to have children. This is why feminism is so important today.

Who were the Suffragettes?

At the turn of the twentieth century, a group of women – who became known as the Suffragettes – campaigned for women to have the right to vote. Suffragettes in the UK used many forms of protest including chaining themselves to railings, marching on London and setting fire to letterboxes. Many women were sent to jail and refused to eat. During the First World War, the protestors turned their cause into support for the troops. This won them public favour and, in 1918, British women over thirty who owned a home were granted

AMERICAN SUFFRAGETTES PROTESTING OUTSIDE THE WHITE HOUSE IN 1918

" I [...] think it is right I am paid the same as my male counterparts. I think it is right that I should be able to make decisions about my own body. I think it is right that women be involved on my behalf in the policies and decision-making of my country. I think it is right that socially, I am afforded the same respect as men. "

EMMA WATSON, ACTOR

the vote. Similar campaigns took place in the US and in 1920 American women were granted the right to vote.

In some parts of the world, women still don't have those fundamental human rights. Recently, women all over the world marched in protest at their rights being threatened.

A feminist is someone who thinks that women should have the same rights and opportunities that men have. Feminists can be women and men; it's anyone who wants things to be fair.

What is sexism?

Sexism is the belief that members of one sex, usually women, are less skilful or intelligent than those of the other sex. Sexist behaviours and attitudes try to decide what women can or can't do, just because of their sex.

Some schools and universities now have Feminism Societies to highlight sexism where there is still unfairness. Lots of famous celebrities describe themselves as feminists: Beyoncé, Taylor Swift, Mark Ruffalo, John Legend and Miley Cyrus have all used the 'F-Word' in interviews!

" All men should be feminists. If men care more about women's rights, the world will be a better place. "

JOHN LEGEND, MUSICIAN

Why do we need feminism?

That's a really big question. All around the world both boys and girls are suffering in lots of different ways: poverty, illness and exploitation. However, if you happened to be born male your prospects, statistically, are a little rosier.

In 2013, it was estimated that some 63 million girls of school age weren't getting an education. This can be because boys' education, in some countries, is considered more important than that of girls. Sometimes girls are expected to do domestic jobs instead of going to school.

Not all women have: access to quality healthcare; the right to decide whether they want children; safety from abusive relationships.

In cultures where infant boys are more highly regarded, killing female babies or aborting female foetuses is still occurring.

The gender pay gap means that in the UK for every pound a man earns, a woman earns 81p.

An estimated 200 million women and girls have undergone female genital mutilation (FGM) or circumcision (FGC). 137,000 of these were women and girls from the UK. Unlike male circumcision, FGM has serious implications for a woman's life. It is illegal to carry out FGM in the UK or to take a girl abroad to have it.

There are more men called John in charge of the UK's one hundred biggest companies than there are women bosses altogether.

While we still have inequality – and inequality that mostly affects women – we need the word feminism.

THINK ABOUT

What things could make your school fairer for girls and boys?

" We have to teach our boys the rules of equality and respect, so that as they grow up, gender equality becomes a natural way of life. And we have to teach our girls that they can reach as high as humanly possible. **"**

BEYONCÉ KNOWLES-CARTER

My gender:

Holly Bourne

Holly Bourne is the bestselling author of The Spinster Club, a trilogy of books for young adults celebrating feminism and female friendship.

Being a girl

So there are some totally brilliant things about being a girl. On a shallow level, just the pure CHOICE OF OUTFITS and the excitement of trying out a new lipstick. And, on a more meaningful level, the incredibly deep but hilarious friendships you make with other girls. But there are also lots of downsides.

Feeling like you should be pretty. All the time.

If I try and combine all the things we're told a girl *should* look like, I think it comes to this. You must be thin, with cellulite-free thighs that do not touch at the top, and with boobs that are big but not droopy. Oh, and don't forget the flat stomach. Your skin must be perfectly clear. Your lips full. Your hair must be volumised but not frizzy .... Exhausted yet? Feeling insecure and filled with self-hatred yet?

You have the power

And that's why I write books about fighting back, standing up for what's right, or simply just turning to a friend and saying, 'this feels weird. Does it feel weird to you too?' There's so much power in just talking about all the crazy stuff we're forced to put up with. So, if you ever get a funny feeling in your tummy that something is wrong, grab some friends and have a chat about it. Opening up may not only help you feel better, these sorts of conversations can really change the world.

What is cross-dressing?

Lots of entertainers play with gender stereotypes when they are performing. Sometimes men dress as women and sometimes women dress as men. RuPaul, David Walliams, Matt Lucas, Dame Edna Everage and Lily Savage are some comedy drag queens you might have heard of, as it's very common in theatre and music.

Dressing in drag

'Drag' comes from the days of Shakespeare when it was usual for men to play female roles so would have to 'DRess As a Girl' or 'DR.A.G'.

World-famous pop stars like Lady Gaga, David Bowie, Madonna, Katy Perry, Boy George and Annie Lennox have all experimented with male and female stereotypes as part of their performances.

Drag identity

The difference between a drag queen (or king) and a transgender person is that when the costumes, wigs and make-up comes off, a drag performer still identifies with their birth sex. That's because simply dressing a certain way doesn't define a person's identity – or whether they feel they are a man or a woman.

"... I portray myself in a very androgynous way, and I love androgyny. "

LADY GAGA

RuPaul

RuPaul Charles is perhaps the most famous drag queen in the whole world. He started out as a personality in a New York City performance club before releasing albums and appearing in movies during the nineties. These days, he's best known as the host of *RuPaul's Drag Race*, a reality show which has very much brought drag culture into the mainstream with millions of fans worldwide.

'Drag is about mocking identity. Drag is really about reminding people that you are more than you think you are – you are more than what it says on your passport.'

What is a transvestite?

A transvestite is someone who enjoys wearing clothes traditionally assigned to the opposite sex. They are also sometimes called 'cross-dressers'. Unlike a drag king or queen, a transvestite might cross-dress in their daily life, not just as part of a performance.

❚ It doesn't matter what sex or sexuality, how you identify or who you fancy ... What do you do in life? What do you add to the human existence – that is what matters. ❚

EDDIE IZZARD, COMEDIAN

Gender
around the world

We've already talked about how gender is nowhere near as simple as 'boy or girl', 'man or woman', and all over the world, different cultures regard gender in different ways. Here are just some of the cultures who recognise more than two genders.

Native Americans spiritually acknowledge **Two-Spirit** people. Many Native American groups recognise four genders: feminine woman, masculine woman, feminine man and masculine man.

The indigenous **Māhū** of Hawaii are people who have both male and female traits. Unlike transgender people their identity is more fluid, existing between male and female.

The **Sworn Virgins** of Albania are born female but swear an oath to live and work as men. This practice, which is now dying out, was a way for females to have the same rights as men.

The **Hijra** of India, Pakistan and Bangladesh have been part of South Asian culture for thousands of years. In India Hijra is recognised as an offical 'third gender'.

Born male, the **Kathoeys** of Thailand are recognised by many Thai people as the nation's 'third gender'. Some schools even have toilets for three genders, not just two.

The **Fa'afafine** of Samoa have been a recognised third gender since at least the early 20th century. 'Fa'afafine' translates as 'in the manner of a woman'.

What's the difference between sex and sexuality?

Sex and sexuality are two unrelated concepts. Sex – in its very most basic terms – comes down to whether you ARE a boy or a girl. Sexuality, again very simplistically, is whether you FANCY boys or girls. See? Easy, huh? People are attracted to people for all sorts of reasons and there's not a lot you can do about it! You just fancy who you fancy!

" Sexuality is who you are personally attracted to ... But gender identity is who you are in your soul. "

CAITLYN JENNER, AMERICAN TV PERSONALITY

Describing your identity

Sexual identity is a bit like gender identity in that it's about defining yourself according to how you feel at any given time. Some people change their sexual identity as they move through life, and that's fine. Sometimes people choose a label which they feel best describes their sexual identity. You may have heard of:

- Straight or heterosexual: when you're attracted to someone of the opposite gender as you.

- Gay, lesbian or homosexual: when you're attracted to someone with the same gender as you.

- Bisexual or pansexual: a bisexual person is someone who is attracted to both men and women while a pansexual is attracted to people regardless of their gender.

- Asexual: asexual people often aren't sexually attracted to people at all, but this doesn't mean they won't have boyfriends or girlfriends – it just means sex isn't a big factor in their relationships.

There are lots of ways to define your sexual identity and some people prefer not to attach labels to themselves at all.

Some people still worry about being lesbian, gay or bisexual (LGB) and think their friends and family won't accept their sexuality. LGB people are still discriminated against and sometimes unfairly face mockery. It can be difficult to tell people about your identity, but most LGB people find that, when they 'come out' most people are very understanding.

Being LGB is nothing to be ashamed of. If you have concerns about your sexual identity, there is more support at the back of this book.

THINK ABOUT

Why do you think people label their identities? How important is having a sense of self?

LOVE

PRIDE

My gender:
Matt Lister

Matt Lister is a model and writer from London. He competed as a canoe slalom athlete for Great Britain for over 10 years.

How long have you known you were gay?

I always knew I was gay, for as long as I can remember. From the moment I became attracted to anyone else I've always been attracted to men. When I get asked, 'So how long have you known?' my answer is that I guess I always have.

School years

Whilst I was at school, I was chubby, spotty and rubbish at all the sports we had to do in PE other than gymnastics and trampolining. There were already a couple of others in my year that had come out as gay, lesbian or bisexual, but the mixed reactions of the other kids terrified me. I decided I was just going to ride out my years at school and when I left, that was my time to just be honest and be myself.

Testing the waters

When I turned 17 I told a close friend, then a closer friend. I guess I was testing the water, building up to the big ones. Then I told my sister. There was a good 2–3 minutes of '... REALLY?!'. But the next part of that was 'you have to tell mum and dad because I can't keep this a secret.'

Coming out

A little later on, into my sporting career, I began competing internationally and was exposed to a whole new world where I felt even more that I couldn't truly be myself. I was scared that coming out would somehow damage my chances of achieving my goals and dreams in sport, but during my career it was the opposite. When I came out, I felt free on the water and my results improved. I was the first British athlete to be selected in two disciplines for the national team and I gained many medals. I was invited to commentate at world cups and the world championships.

LGBT support

In 2015 I was contacted by the British Athletes Commission asking me if I thought there was something they could do to support their LGBT (lesbian, gay, bisexual, transgender) athletes better. This led to me being appointed LGBT Athlete Ambassador for British Athletes. This was the first ever role of its kind for a player's association.

Looking back

I wish I had had the courage to be honest with my friends and family earlier about being gay. I'd love the opportunity to go back and talk to my younger self, tell little Matt that it's all going to be ok.

Do we need gender?

If gender causes nothing but trouble and strife, why do we bother? Well, whether we like it or not, society is still very gendered so it's hard to avoid. Some people might say it's about trying to make yourself look attractive, or simply follow fashion. Other people say they dress and look however they want because it makes them happy. Some enjoy the brotherhood or sisterhood of belonging to a gender. Some people don't give it very much thought at all!

What is genderfluid, genderqueer or gender non-binary?

❚ Gender fluidity is not really feeling like you're at one end of the spectrum or the other. For the most part, I definitely don't identify as any gender. I'm not a guy; I don't really feel like a woman, but obviously I was born one. So, I'm somewhere in the middle, which – in my perfect imagination – is like having the best of both sexes. ❚

RUBY ROSE, ACTOR

" I saw one human in particular who didn't identify as male or female. Looking at them, they were both: beautiful and sexy and tough but vulnerable and feminine but masculine. And I related to that person more than I related to anyone in my life. "

MILEY CYRUS, SINGER

Some people are convinced gender is a load of silly nonsense, or they simply feel neither like a boy or a girl. They might use a label like genderfluid, genderqueer or gender non-binary. Instead of using 'he', 'his', 'she' or 'her', they might use the pronoun 'they'. Celebrity chef Jack Monroe and pop star Miley Cyrus both identify as gender neutral.

WHO CARES?

" I want to be treated as a person. Not as a woman or a man. "

JACK MONROE

My gender:
Krishna Istha

Krishna Istha is a live artist and performance maker from the UK. They are interested in pop culture representation, and their work focuses on themes of queer culture, gender politics and feminism.

I am an artist and work in the theatre. I like wearing skirts and blue nail polish, and I have really short hair that is often cut in funky patterns.

I am genderqueer and, to me, that means that I feel like a boy some days, and like a girl some days and a mixture of both most days! You could also describe my gender as 'multi-gender'. Sometimes it's hard to explain my gender to people, because they are used to thinking of everyone as either boys or girls, but there's many of us that are neither or both.

In Indian mythology, there's loads of gods, goddess and other-worldly beings that are depicted as trans, and they transform from one gender to another and back over time and that is kind of how I feel on a daily basis.

Most people create their own version of gender, a version that suits them. Being a boy or being a girl can mean different things to different people. We all take elements of gender stereotypes and make them work for us or defy them entirely.

My gender: Andrew McMillan

Andrew McMillan is an award-winning British poet. He currently lectures in creative writing.

I came out to my parents when I was 16. I'd known I was gay probably since I was about 14, but never had a language to explain what it was I was feeling – we never got taught about same-sex relationships in school. All I knew was I'd been given this body, this masculinity, this feeling when I was born and I didn't know what it was, but I knew it wasn't what it was for a lot of other boys in my school. This poem is a way of thinking about how we might feel there's a certain expectation on us to be a certain way, and how we might challenge that.

Watch

when I was first born
my father gave me
a watch   I didn't
have a use for it
at first   never thought

of it   when I was
five or six I asked
what it was   was told
*it's something for when
you're older*   my parents

called it important
and I felt the weight
of it as I grew
but it looked old
didn't suit my style

and when I was ten
maybe eleven
I told my mother
I didn't want it
that this thing I had

been given made me
uncomfortable
but it was your dad's
she said   *before that
it was your grandad's*

but I still refused
and she relented
told me that it was
my choice   and she would
tell my father too

and he   realising it was a
different time
wanted me to choose my
own   and was also fine

What's your gender?

male
female
non-binary
transgender
intersex

? ? ? ? ?

Hopefully I've given you a lot to think about. This book might have got you thinking about YOUR gender too. Some BIG QUESTIONS you might be asking are:

- What is MY gender?

- Do I feel more like a boy or a girl?

- What do I like about being a girl/a boy?

- What does it actually mean to 'feel like a boy' or 'feel like a girl'?

- Do I like stereotypical clothes, toys or activities?

- Have I experienced sexism?

- Am I attracted to boys, girls, neither or both?

- Am I a feminist?

Asking yourself BIG QUESTIONS, especially when you're young, is perfectly natural.

Here's another thing: your identity will change and evolve over time.

" A gender-equal society would be one where the word 'gender' does not exist: where everyone can be themselves. "

GLORIA STEINEM, AUTHOR

It happens to everyone. How you feel now, might not be how you feel in five or ten years' time. People change all the time, whether we like it or not! Part of growing up is re-evaluating your feelings about yourself.

However you identify, rest assured it's the most natural thing in the world. All you can ever be is yourself, and the most honest, authentic version of you is completely glorious!

Gender terminology

Assigned gender – the gender given to you as a baby based on your external genitals at birth. This assigned gender will affect how a baby is reared because of gender norms, such as the clothes a child wears and the toys they are given to play with.

Cisgender – the term used for someone whose gender identity is the same as their assigned gender.

Gender binary – a gender system where sex is classified into two distinct groups: male and female.

Genderfluid – a description of a person who identifies with neither, both or a combination of male and female genders. A person who is genderfluid always feels a mix between traditional genders but may feel more female on one day and more male the next.

Gender non-binary – a gender system that is neither male or female but recognises other genders, such as genderfluid.

Genderqueer – a term used to describe any gender identities other than male and female.

Intersex – the term given to a person whose physical characteristics at birth were neither male or female. Medical staff at the birth would therefore be unable to assign a gender.

LGBTQ – an acronym which stands for Lesbian Gay Bisexual Transgender Queer/Questioning. It is used to denote a community of people whose gender identities often bring about shared political and social concerns.

Third gender – the recognition in some cultures that there can be more than two genders (male and female) and a third gender exists. Some people can be defined as neither a man or a woman.

Trans – an all-encompassing term given to anyone who would define themselves as transgender, transsexual, both male and female, neither male or female, androgynous or a third gender.

Transgender – a person whose gender identity is different to the gender they were assigned at birth. FTM means female to male, and refers to someone who was assigned female at birth but who identifies as male. MTF means male to female, and refers to someone who was assigned male at birth but who identifies as female.

Transvestite – refers to a person who enjoys dressing in clothes and make-up usually associated with people from the opposite sex.

" I love to be individual, to step beyond gender. "

ANNIE LENNOX, SINGER

Helpful numbers and websites

Childline: A helpline and listening service for young people. Live 24/7, a call to Childline is free and won't show up on your phone bill.
0800 1111

Feminista UK: Found out how to set up a feminism club or run a campaign at school.
ukfeminista.org.uk

Gender Identity Research and Education Society: GIRES' purpose is to improve the lives of trans and gender non-conforming people, including those who are non-binary and non-gender. It gives a voice to trans and gender non-conforming individuals, including those who are non-binary and non-gender, as well as their families. **www.gires.org.uk**

Gendered Intelligence: Advice and support for young transgender people and their families.
genderedintelligence.co.uk

Mermaids UK: Help and support for trans youth and their families.
mermaidsuk.org.uk

The Mix: Support and advice for under 25s. The Mix is the UK's leading support service for young people. They provide anything from mental health to money, from homelessness to finding a job, from break-ups to drugs. **themix.org.uk**
0808 808 4994

Switchboard LGBT: A helpline service for LGBTQ people open from 10 am to 10 pm every day.
0300 330 0630

UK Trans Info: A national charity focused on improving the lives of trans and non-binary people in the UK. **uktrans.info**

Glossary

ambiguous something that could have than one interpretation or meaning

androgynous partly male and partly female in appearance

'come out' to openly declare your sexuality

characteristic a feature or quality belonging to a person

chromosomes thread-like structures found in most cells in the human body, which carry genetic information, such as a person's sex

circumcision the practice of cutting off the foreskin on a boy's penis for religious, or sometimes medical reasons. In girls, the clitoris and sometimes the labia are cut off as a traditional practice among some peoples, but female circumcision is less common

evolving developing gradually

feminism supporting women's rights on the grounds of equality for all sexes

gender the state of feeling like the member of one sex or another

gender transition the change from one gender to another, undertaken when a person is unhappy with their assigned gender at birth

genitals the human reproductive organs that are outside the body

hormones a chemical produced by the body, or taken as medicine, that stimulates certain cells into a specific action

human rights a right which is believed to belong to every person regardless of background, culture, gender or skin colour

identity the fact of being who or what a person is

indigenous originating from a particular place

objectify to degrade somebody to the status of an object instead of a person

pronoun a word used to refer to someone in a sentence e.g. he, she

sex either of two main categories (male and female) into which humans are divided according to their reproductive organs

sexism the unfair treatment of people, especially women, because of their sex;

sexuality the ability to have sexual feelings for somebody else

social construct an idea that has been created and accepted by a society

stereotype a widely held and fixed idea of a particular type of person and what they should be or how they should behave

Index